Recover

Codependency

Dale & Juanita Ryan

6 Studies for
Groups or Individuals

With Notes for Leaders

◣ *LIFE RECOVERY GUIDES*

INTERVARSITY PRESS
DOWNERS GROVE, ILLINOIS 60515

InterVarsity Press is the book-publishing division of InterVarsity Christian Fellowship, a student movement active on campus at hundreds of universities, colleges and schools of nursing in the United States of America, and a member movement of the International Fellowship of Evangelical Students. For information about local and regional activities, write Public Relations Dept., InterVarsity Christian Fellowship, 6400 Schroeder Rd., P.O. Box 7895, Madison, WI 53707-7895.

All Scripture quotations, unless otherwise indicated, are from the Holy Bible, New International Version. Copyright © 1973, 1978, International Bible Society. Used by permission of Zondervan Bible Publishers.

Cover illustration: Tim Nyberg

ISBN 0-8308-1156-7

Printed in the United States of America

12	11	10	9	8	7	6	5	4	
99	98	97	96	95	94	93	92	91	

An Invitation to Recovery   5

Recovering from Codependency   11

1   Letting Go of Over-Responsibility   14
    Exodus 18:13-24

2   Letting God Give Us Rest   19
    Matthew 11:28-30

3   Letting Go of Denial   24
    Psalm 102:1-11, 17-20

4   Letting God Help Us Tell the Truth   30
    Matthew 18:15-17

5   Letting Go of Blame   35
    Genesis 3:1-13

6   Letting God Take Care of Those We Love   41
    Mark 10:17-23

Leader's Notes   47

An Invitation to Recovery

Life Recovery Guides are rooted in four basic convictions.

First, we are in need of recovery. The word *recovery* implies that something has gone wrong. Things are not as they should be. We have sinned. We have been sinned against. We are entangled, stuck, bogged down, bound and broken. We need to be healed.

Second, recovery is a commitment to change. Because of this, recovery is a demanding process and often a lengthy one. There are no quick fixes in recovery. It means facing the truth about ourselves, even when that truth is painful. It means giving up our old destructive patterns and learning new life-giving patterns. Recovery means taking responsibility for our lives. It is not easy. It is sometimes painful. And it will take time.

Third, recovery is possible. No matter how hopeless it may seem, no matter how deeply we have been wounded by life or how often we have failed, recovery is possible. Our primary basis for hope in the process of recovery is that God is able to do things which we cannot do ourselves. Recovery is possible because God has committed himself to us.

Finally, these studies are rooted in the conviction that the Bible can be a significant resource for recovery. Many people who have lived through difficult life experiences have had bits of the Bible thrown at their pain as a quick fix or a simplistic solution. As a result, many people expect the Bible to be a barrier to recovery rather than a resource. These studies are based on the belief that the Bible is not a book of quick fixes and simplistic solutions. It is, on the contrary, a practical and helpful resource for recovery.

We were deeply moved personally by these biblical texts as we worked on this series. We are convinced that the God of the Bible can bring serenity to people whose lives have become unmanageable. If you are looking for resources to help you in your recovery, we invite you to study the Bible with an open mind and heart.

Getting the Most from Life Recovery Guides

Life Recovery Guides are designed to assist you to find out for yourself what the Bible has to say about different aspects of recovery. The texts you will study will be thought-provoking, challenging, inspiring and very personal. It will become obvious that these studies are not designed merely to convince you of the truthfulness of some idea. Rather, they are designed to allow biblical truths to renew your heart and mind.

We want to encourage realistic expectations of these discussion guides. First, they are not intended to be everything-the-Bible-says about any subject. They are not intended to be a systematic presentation of biblical theology.

Second, we want to emphasize that these guides are not intended to provide a recovery program or to be a substitute for professional counseling. If you are in a counseling relationship or are involved in a support group, we pray that these studies will enrich that resource. If you are not in a counseling relationship and your recovery involves long-term issues, we encourage you to consider seeking the assistance of a mental health professional.

What these guides are designed to do is to help you study a series of biblical texts which relate to the process of recovery. Our hope is that they will allow you to discover the Good News for people who are struggling to recover.

There are six studies in each Life Recovery Guide. This should provide you with maximum flexibility in how you use these guides. Combining the guides in various ways will allow you to adapt them to your time schedule and to focus on the concerns most important to you or your group.

All of the studies in this series use a workbook format. Space is provided for writing answers to each question. This is ideal for personal study and allows group members to prepare in advance for the discussion. The guides also contain leader's notes with suggestions on how to lead a group discussion. The notes provide additional background information on certain questions, give helpful tips on group dynamics and suggest ways to deal with problems that may arise during the discussion. These features enable someone with little or no experience to lead an effective discussion.

Suggestions for Individual Study

1. As you begin each study, pray that God would bring healing and recovery to you through his Word.

2. After spending time in personal reflection, read and reread the passage to be studied.

3. Write your answers in the spaces provided or in a personal journal. Writing can bring clarity and deeper understanding of yourself and of the Bible. For the same reason, we suggest that you write out your prayers at the end of each study.

4. Use the leader's notes at the back of the guide to gain additional insight and information.

5. Share what you are learning with someone you trust. Recovery is empowered by experiences of community.

Suggestions for Group Study

Even if you have already done these studies individually, we strongly encourage you to find some way to do them with a group of other people as well. Although each person's recovery is different, everyone's recovery is empowered by the mutual support and encouragement that can only be found in a one-on-one or a group setting. Several reminders may be helpful for participants in a group study:

1. Realize that trust grows over time. If opening up in a group setting is risky, realize that you do not have to share more than what feels safe to you. However, taking risks is a necessary part of recovery. So, do participate in the discussion as much as you are able.

2. Be sensitive to the other members of the group. Listen attentively when they talk. You will learn from their insights. If you can, link what you say to the comments of others so the group stays on the topic. Also, be affirming whenever you can. This will encourage some of the more hesitant members of the group to participate.

3. Be careful not to dominate the discussion. We are sometimes so eager to share what we have learned that we do not leave opportunity for others to respond. By all means participate! But allow others to do so as well.

4. Expect God to teach you through the passage being discussed and through the other members of the group. Pray that you will have a profitable time together.

5. We recommend that groups follow a few basic guidelines, and that these guidelines be read at the beginning of each discussion session. The guidelines, which you may wish to adapt to your situation, are:

a. Anything said in the group is considered confidential and will not be discussed outside the group unless specific permission is given to do so.

b. We will provide time for each person present to talk if he or she feels comfortable doing so.

c. We will talk about ourselves and our own situations, avoiding conversation about other people.

d. We will listen attentively to each other.

e. We will be very cautious about giving advice.

   f. We will pray for each other.

If you are the discussion leader, you will find additional suggestions and helpful ideas for each study in the leader's notes. These are found at the back of the guide.

Recovering from Codependency

"Cast all your care on him, because he cares for you" (1 Peter 5:7).

This is simple, but good, advice for people who are anxious and frantic about life. We can give our worries to God. We can trust him with our cares, because he loves us. No one needs this advice more than people who are caught up in the anxious and frantic confusion that comes from codependent behavior.

Codependent behaviors are panic reactions to another person's addiction or compulsion. The fear, anger and helplessness a person feels when someone they love is addicted can lead to desperate attempts to "take care of" or control the loved one. Unfortunately, these behaviors are not helpful. Instead, both the addicted person's behavior and the frenzied codependent behavior combine in a destructive downward cycle.

The studies in this guide focus on three aspects of breaking the cycle of codependent behavior. We can (1) let go of over-responsibility and let God give us rest, (2) let go of denial and let God help us tell the truth, and (3) let go of blame and let God take care of the person we love.

People who become entangled in the web of codependency often have a long history of over-responsibility. Codependency is rooted in a drive to do it all, and to do it perfectly. Typically, codependents have learned that their only value in life is derived from what they do, rather than from who they are. As a result, they are driven to do too much—so much, in fact, that no time remains to focus on their own needs or to rest in God's love. One aspect of recovery from codependency, then, is to let go of over-responsibility and let God give us rest.

Codependent behavior is also rooted in an active denial of life's problems and of the painful emotions which accompany these problems. People who are ensnared by codependency can sustain their denial even while making desperate, private attempts to "fix" what is seen as the "problem." Denial leaves a person isolated, afraid, exhausted, angry and confused but determined to try even harder to find a solution. Solutions remain elusive, however, because the denial keeps the full range of problems from being acknowledged or addressed. Recovery from codependency requires that we let go of denial and let God help us to tell the truth.

Finally, codependent behavior is rooted in the belief that happiness in life is a direct result of other people's behavior. As a result, a person reasons that to be happy, they need to control the behavior of the people closest to them. Controlling behaviors include a wide range of activities. A person may yell and lecture, accuse and blame, withhold love and affection, or work very, very hard to please the other person in the hope that they can "earn" the right to control. The problem is, of course, that it is not possible to control other people. Attempts to do so only make us more and more miserable. This misery is then blamed on the people we are trying to control. Recovery from codependency requires that we let go of blame and that we learn instead to entrust the people we love to the care of God.

"Let go and let God." It's a simple slogan. It is not, however, an easy process. Letting go of over-responsibility seems like it will result in terrible chaos. Letting go of denial means facing painful truths and grieving painful losses. Letting go of blame means experiencing loss of power.

Letting go and letting God is a frightening and risky adventure. But it is a journey which leads to serenity. We can let go of our cares. We can cast them on God. He cares for us.

Our prayer is that these studies will encourage you to take the next step in your recovery. May God grant you the courage to let go and let God.

May your roots sink deeply in the soil of God's love.

Dale and Juanita Ryan

1
Letting Go of Over-Responsibility

"If I don't do it, it won't get done right. Someone has to do it, I guess it'll have to be me."

This is the voice of the codependent person who has learned to be responsible for everything. It's not just that we are responsible people—that would be fine. It's that we are universally responsible. Inappropriately responsible. Compulsively responsible. Sometimes, we are even offensively responsible.

The central myth that feeds over-responsibility is "If I don't do it, no one will." A strong supporting role is played by the perfectionist's myth: "Even if others would do it, they wouldn't get it right." The logical consequence of these myths is "I have to do it, and I have to do it all." This is, of course, a burden too heavy for any mortal.

Being over-responsible keeps us very busy. We can get lost in the endless demands associated with other people's problems. We become martyrs—often angry, exhausted martyrs who are unable to comprehend why people are not grateful for our hard work.

Letting go of over-responsibility is not easy for people who struggle with codependence. It is difficult to face our limits. It is difficult to give up our myths. It is difficult to trust other people to be responsible and helpful. It is difficult to learn that we are not God. However, that is precisely what the Christian faith requires. It requires us to confess that God is God. And we are not.

☐ **Personal Reflection** ————————————————————

1. Make a list of all the people, activities and tasks you feel responsible for at this time in your life.

2. What thoughts and feelings do you have as you look at this list?

☐ **Bible Study** ————————————————————————

Moses took his seat to serve as judge for the people, and they stood around him from morning till evening. When his father-in-law saw all that Moses was doing for the people, he said, "What is this you are doing for the people? Why do you alone sit as judge, while all these people stand around you from morning till evening?"

Moses answered him, "Because the people come to me to seek God's will. Whenever they have a dispute, it is brought to me, and

I decide between the parties and inform them of God's decrees and laws."

Moses' father-in-law replied, "What you are doing is not good. You and these people who come to you will only wear yourselves out. The work is too heavy for you; you cannot handle it alone. Listen now to me and I will give you some advice, and may God be with you. You must be the people's representative before God and bring their disputes to him. Teach them the decrees and laws, and show them the way to live and the duties they are to perform. But select capable men from all the people—men who fear God, trustworthy men who hate dishonest gain—and appoint them as officials over thousands, hundreds, fifties and tens. Have them serve as judges for the people at all times, but have them bring every difficult case to you; the simple cases they can decide themselves. That will make your load lighter, because they will share it with you. If you do this and God so commands, you will be able to stand the strain, and all the people will go home satisfied."

Moses listened to his father-in-law and did everything he said. (Exodus 18:13-24)

_____

1. What insights did you gain during your time of personal reflection?

2. What problems did Jethro see in Moses' leadership?

3. What do you think about the way Jethro presents his concerns to Moses?

4. What does Moses' initial response to Jethro suggest about his perspective on why he was doing all of the work?

5. What losses might Moses have experienced as he took Jethro's advice and gave up being over-responsible?

6. What benefits do you think came out of the changes Moses made?

7. In what ways do you relate to Moses' over-responsibility in this story?

8. What makes it difficult for you to follow Moses' example of letting go of over-responsibility?

9. What could give you the courage to begin to follow Moses' example?

☐ **Prayer** ——————————————————————————————

Finish the following prayer: "God, I need your help to let go of being over-responsible for

——————————————————————————————."

2
Letting God
Give Us
Rest

"It's O.K. It's not that bad. I can manage, thanks. I wouldn't actually
say I'm burdened, I just get a little tired sometimes."

Those of us who are caught up in codependent behavior take on
enormous responsibilities but rarely think of ourselves as burdened.
This apparent high level of functioning is not, unfortunately, a result
of the fact that we are so resourceful and strong that the things
which burden other people don't bother us. It is, rather, that we are
not aware, or not willing to admit, how burdened we are.

Recovery from codependent behavior requires that we face and
experience the burdens of life. We can't release our burdens into
God's care if we don't have any burdens to release. We won't ask for
God's help as long as we believe we can manage on our own.

The text for this study presents a fundamental Christian claim.
There is, Christians insist, some very good news for people who are
willing to face the fact that we are all "burdened." The good news
is that, when we come to the end of our pretense and denial, God
invites us to bring our burdens to him.

God does not demand that we manage or resolve our burdens. We don't need to have everything under control. We can simply come to God. He will be gentle with us. And we will find rest for our souls.

☐ **Personal Reflection** _____

1. What benefits do you experience when you allow yourself to rest?

2. What keeps you from allowing yourself to rest?

3. What burdens are you aware of carrying today?

☐ **Bible Study** _____

"Come to me, all you who are weary and burdened, and I will give you rest. Take my yoke upon you and learn from me, for I am gentle and humble in heart, and you will find rest for your souls. For my yoke is easy and my burden is light." (Matthew 11:28-30)

1. What insights did you gain during your time of personal reflection?

2. Jesus invites weary and burdened people to come to him. What thoughts and feelings do you have in response to this invitation?

3. With Jesus' invitation comes the promise of rest. For people caught up in codependent behaviors the possibility of rest is full of anxiety. Is there something about resting that makes you anxious? Explain why or why not.

4. Jesus describes himself as one who is "gentle and humble in heart." How would believing this about Jesus help you to rest in his presence?

5. Jesus says that his yoke is easy and his burden light. How would believing this about Jesus help you to accept rest from him?

6. Think of a positive image of rest (a cat curled in the sun, an infant sleeping, a hiker sitting by a stream). Picture yourself as the one resting in the scene. Now, imagine that you are resting in Jesus' presence.

What response do you have to this image of rest?

7. This invitation from Jesus shows us a dramatic picture of God's care for us. Remembering that God cares for us can help us to find the courage to trust him to carry our burdens. How have you seen God care for you in the past?

8. Write down the cares that are most burdensome to you today. Next to each of your cares write down one feature of God's character (for example, God is gentle, or God is attentive) that would give you reason to see God as someone who could be trusted with carrying each particular burden.

What perspective did you gain during this exercise?

□ **Prayer** ————————————————————————————

Finish the following prayer: "God, help me to come, help me to rest, help me to trust you to carry

———————————————————————————."

3
Letting Go
of
Denial

We dress up when we go to church, and we smile a lot. As long as no one comes to the house, no one really knows that things aren't going well. Actually, things aren't so bad really. I'm sure that I'll eventually figure out some way to fix whatever is wrong.

Denial is incredibly difficult to get rid of because it protects us from certain kinds of emotional pain. Letting go of denial means that we will see reality for what it is and that we will experience all of the painful emotions which denial has so effectively allowed us to avoid.

Letting go of denial is, however, an essential step in recovery. It is a step we take many times over as, bit by bit, we face new truths about ourselves and our lives.

The prayers of the psalms can be used to facilitate the process of letting go of denial. The author of the psalms gives voice to his pain and distress. He models for us the kind of honest self-disclosure that makes recovery possible.

☐ Personal Reflection ————————————

1. What experiences have you had with letting go of denial?

2. What emotions did you experience as you let yourself face the truth?

3. What benefits do you see in letting go of denial?

☐ Bible Study ————————————————

Hear my prayer, O LORD;
    let my cry for help come to you.
Do not hide your face from me
    when I am in distress.

Turn your ear to me;
    when I call, answer me quickly.

For my days vanish like smoke;
    my bones burn like glowing embers.
  My heart is blighted and withered like grass;
    I forget to eat my food.
Because of my loud groaning
    I am reduced to skin and bones.

I am like a desert owl,
    like an owl among the ruins.
I lie awake; I have become
    like a bird alone on a roof.
All day long my enemies taunt me;
    those who rail against me use my name as a curse.
For I eat ashes as my food
    and mingle my drink with tears
because of your great wrath,
    for you have taken me up and thrown me aside.
My days are like the evening shadow;
    I wither away like grass.

He will respond to the prayer of the destitute;
    he will not despise their plea.
Let this be written for a future generation,
    that a people not yet created may praise the Lord:
"The LORD looked down from his sanctuary on high,
    from heaven he viewed the earth,
to hear the groans of the prisoners
    and release those condemned to death."
(Psalm 102:1-11, 17-20)

1. What insights did you gain during your time of personal reflection?

2. The author of this psalm describes himself as being in distress and having a heart that is "blighted and withered like grass." How is this like the experience of a person caught up in codependent behavior?

3. We read: "I am like an owl among the ruins. I lie awake. I have become like a bird alone on a roof." How is this like the experience of a person who is caught up in codependent behavior?

4. In the last sentences, the author compares his experience to that of a prisoner condemned to death. In what ways might codependent behavior lead a person to feel like a prisoner condemned to death?

5. Which of the other descriptions of distress resemble the experience of codependency?

6. The writer says to God, "because of your great wrath . . . you have taken me up and thrown me aside." It is important to remember that God does not "throw us aside" in wrath, even though past experiences of abuse may lead many codependent people to fear this about God. What in the experience of codependence can lead a person to feel that God has thrown them aside?

7. In spite of sometimes feeling like God has discarded him, the writer finds courage in remembering God's compassion. He says that God "will respond to the prayers of the destitute." What experiences have you had with God responding to your prayers when you felt destitute?

8. Facing the truth about our situations in life will involve experiencing pain. Try picturing your denial as a series of prison bars.

You are trapped inside, alone with your terror and confusion. Picture God coming to you and one by one removing the bars of your cell. He offers you his presence as you face the reality of your past and present. He offers you comfort as you grieve the pain in your life. He offers you freedom, as you let him remove the bars of denial from your heart and mind.

What thoughts and feelings did you have during this meditation?

□ Prayer ————————————————————————————

Finish the following prayer: "God, help me to let go of my denial and face the pain about

_____."

4
Letting God Help Us Tell the Truth

"It really doesn't matter. I hardly noticed. I didn't mind. It wasn't anything."

An adjective that can be used to describe codependent behavior is nice. "Nice" in this context refers to persons who minimize the extent of the hurt they experience, or deny the problem all together.

The goal of recovery is not to become socially rude or inappropriate. It is, however, important to learn how dysfunctional "nice" can be. Being nice means that problems go unaddressed and unresolved. The emotional damage associated with hurts is buried. Relationships are slowly eroded away by unspoken anger. Problems continue because they are never faced directly. Being nice may feel safe and may even feel "Christian" to many people. The reality is that "nice" is often a lie. It is often a cover for deep hurt and anger.

As we let go of denial, we can begin to let God help us tell the truth. Letting God help us tell the truth may mean that we will have to give up the security of being nice. We will have to face the problems that exist in our relationships. We will have to experience the hurt and anger we have been afraid to acknowledge directly.

Telling the truth does not mean that we have to compulsively confront every problem. It means that we need to respect the people close to us enough to tell them when we have been significantly hurt by their behavior. We need to stop pretending it doesn't matter when it does matter. We need to offer them the opportunity to know how their behavior impacts us.

☐ **Personal Reflection** ━━━━━━━━━━━━━━━━━━━━━━━━━━━━━

1. Think of times when you needed to tell someone that they had hurt you. What was the behavior that was hurtful to you?

2. What did you do (or not do)?

3. What were the results of your behavior in response to the hurt?

☐ **Bible Study**━━━━━━━━━━━━━━━━━━━━━━━━━━━━━━━━━

If your brother sins against you, go and show him his fault, just between the two of you. If he listens to you, you have won your brother over. But if he will not listen, take one or two others along, so that "every matter may be established by the testimony of two or three witnesses." If he refuses to listen to them, tell it to the church; and if he refuses to listen even to the church, treat him as you would a pagan or a tax collector. (Matthew 18:15-17)

---

1. What insights did you gain during your time of personal reflection?

2. Codependency leads people to minimize, pretend and deny when they have been hurt. Jesus, by contrast, teaches the importance of direct, honest communication even in difficult situations. What wisdom do his words provide about telling the truth when we have been hurt?

3. Many of us have learned to talk *about* people when they have hurt us, but we have not learned to talk *with* the person who has hurt us. What potential damage can result from talking about a person rather than with them?

4. What makes direct, honest communication so difficult when we are hurt?

5. What are the potential advantages to both parties in starting with a direct, honest conversation just between the two of you?

6. What are the advantages of involving others in attempts at reconciliation?

7. Jesus' audience understood the traditional role of village leaders in the resolution of conflicts. How might Jesus' advice about involving the church be applied in our culture?

8. If a person refuses to listen even after the involvement of the community of faith, Jesus says we are to treat the person as a pagan or a tax collector. Remembering how Jesus treated pagans and tax collectors, what do you think he meant by this?

9. Discuss which of the following actions would be most helpful to your recovery today:

a. I need to face the fact that I have been hurt.

b. I need to go to the person who hurt me to tell them that I have been hurt.

c. I need to get help, support and counsel, because what I've tried hasn't worked.

d. I need to let go of my demands that the person will apologize or change.

☐ **Prayer** _____

Finish the following prayer: "God, I want to let you help me speak the truth about

_____ ."

5
Letting Go
of
Blame

"I am miserable. It is all your fault. If you would change, I would be happy again."

Codependence is rooted in the belief that our happiness depends on other people's behavior. We believe that in order to be happy, we need to control their behavior. It is not possible, however, to control other people. And when control fails and unhappiness results, we often resort to blame.

People who struggle with codependency sometimes have difficulty distinguishing between telling the truth and blaming. We have difficulty believing that we might be part of the problem. It is other people who need to change—after all, they are the ones who are addicted! And, because it is a way of attempting to control someone's behavior, blaming contributes to the cycle of addiction. Telling the truth requires that we let go of this illusion of control and accept our role in the dynamics of addiction.

Blame is an effective way to keep the focus on other people. By diverting attention from what we need to nourish and sustain our own recovery, blame helps to maintain the status quo in codependent relationships. As a result, blame is destructive to others and very unsatisfying for us.

As the text for this study suggests, blame has been around for a long time. It is one of those fundamental strategies for life that seem useful at the time but which ultimately lead us deeper into dysfunction.

☐ **Personal Reflection** ————————————————————————————

1. What patterns of blame existed in your family of origin? For instance:

Who did the blaming?

Who got blamed?

What was the result?

2. When you find yourself blaming someone else for your unhappiness, what thoughts and feelings usually accompany this blame?

☐ Bible Study————————————————————————

Now the serpent was more crafty than any of the wild animals the Lord God had made. He said to the woman, "Did God really say, 'You must not eat from any tree in the garden'?"

The woman said to the serpent, "We may eat fruit from the trees in the garden, but God did say, 'You must not eat fruit from the tree that is in the middle of the garden, and you must not touch it, or you will die.' "

"You will not surely die," the serpent said to the woman. "For God knows that when you eat of it your eyes will be opened, and you will be like God, knowing good and evil."

When the women saw that the fruit of the tree was good for food and pleasing to the eye, and also desirable for gaining wisdom, she took some and ate it. She also gave some to her husband, who was with her, and he ate it. Then the eyes of both of them were opened, and they realized they were naked; so they sewed fig leaves together and made coverings for themselves.

Then the man and his wife heard the sound of the Lord God as he was walking in the garden in the cool of the day, and they hid from the Lord God among the trees of the garden. But the Lord God called to the man, "Where are you?"

He answered, "I heard you in the garden, and I was afraid because I was naked; so I hid."

And he said, "Who told you that you were naked? Have you eaten from the tree that I commanded you not to eat from?"

The man said, "The woman you put here with me—she gave me some fruit from the tree, and I ate it."

Then the Lord God said to the woman, "What is this you have done?"

The woman said, "The serpent deceived me, and I ate." (Genesis 3:1-13)

1. What insights did you gain during your time of personal reflection?

2. The man and woman did something which God specifically asked them not to do. What immediately followed?

3. What do you think motivated both the man and the woman to blame their behavior on someone else?

4. What problems does blame lead to?

5. Think of a time when you were blamed for something. What was the experience like for you?

6. What makes it difficult to let go of blame?

7. Sometimes in an attempt to avoid blaming others, we fall into the trap of blaming ourselves. How is blaming ourselves different from taking appropriate responsibility for our own behavior?

8. If blaming is destructive, what is constructive?

☐ Prayer —————————————————————————————————

Finish the following prayer: "God, I need your help to let go of blaming

——. "

6
Letting God Take Care of Those We Love

"I can't just sit here and do nothing. He needs me now more than ever. No one understands him like I do. I'm his only hope."

People whose lives are driven by codependency help other people avoid the logical consequences of their behavior. We fix things that other people have broken. We adapt so that other people won't be inconvenienced. We bail people out of jail. We rescue and protect. We believe that other people's behavior and its consequences are our responsibility.

When we learn that all of these behaviors are contributing to problems for others and creating problems for us, we are dismayed. Taking care of consequences for other people has become part of our identity. It has become our primary basis for liking ourselves and for getting others to like us.

For these reasons it is very difficult for us to let God take care of the people we love. When we begin to let go of control and blame, however, we can begin to trust God to be with the people we love as they face the consequences of their behaviors. We can begin to release them, with love, into God's care.

☐ Personal Reflection

1. Think of one or two examples of times when you did something for someone to protect them from the consequences of his or her behavior. Describe what you did.

2. What thoughts and feelings did you have when you did this?

3. What was the result of your efforts to protect the person?

☐ Bible Study

As Jesus started on his way, a man ran up to him and fell on his knees before him. "Good teacher," he asked, "what must I do to inherit eternal life?"

"Why do you call me good?" Jesus answered. "No one is good—except God alone. You know the commandments: 'Do not murder, do not commit adultery, do not steal, do not give false testimony, do not defraud, honor your father and mother.' "

"Teacher," he declared, "all these I have kept since I was a boy."

Jesus looked at him and loved him. "One thing you lack," he said. "Go, sell everything you have and give to the poor, and you will have treasure in heaven. Then come, follow me."

At this the man's face fell. He went away sad, because he had great wealth.

Jesus looked around and said to his disciples, "How hard it is for the rich to enter the kingdom of God!" (Mark 10:17-23).

---

1. What insights did you gain during your time of personal reflection?

2. What do we learn about the man in this story?

3. We read that "Jesus looked at him and loved him." What is your response to this description of Jesus?

4. Jesus invites the man to be his follower, making clear what the

implications would be for him personally. The man "went away sad."
How did Jesus respond to the man's choice?

5. In this story Jesus is rejected by a person he loved. What do you
think Jesus might have felt when the man walked away?

6. In Jesus' place, what might you have wanted to do?

7. Jesus spoke honestly to the man and then allowed him the freedom to walk away. What potential benefits did this behavior have
for the man? What potential risks were there?

8. What makes it difficult for you personally to let the people you love face the consequences of their behavior?

9. Imagine that a person you love makes a choice—in spite of your warning—that you can see will have painful consequences. You want to "soften the blow" by reducing the pain he or she may face. But you don't. Instead you look at the person with love and let him or her go, releasing him or her into God's care.

What were your thoughts and feelings during this meditation?

☐ **Prayer** _____

Finish the following prayer: "God, give me the courage to let you take care of the consequences for

_____."

Leader's Notes

You may be experiencing a variety of feelings as you anticipate leading a group using a Life Recovery Guide. You may feel inadequate and afraid of what will happen. If this is the case, know you are in good company. Many of the kings, prophets and apostles in the Bible felt inadequate and afraid. Many other small group leaders share the experience of fear as well.

Your willingness to lead, however, is a gift to the other group members. It might help if you tell them about your feelings and ask them to pray for you. Keep in mind that the other group members share the responsibility for the group. And realize that it is God's work to bring insight, comfort, healing and recovery to group members. Your role is simply to provide guidance for the discussion. The suggestions listed below will help you to provide that guidance.

Using the Life Recovery Guide Series

This Life Recovery Guide is one in a series of eight guides. The series was designed to be a flexible tool that can be used in various combinations by individuals and groups—such as support groups, Bible studies and Sunday-school classes. Each guide contains six studies. If all eight guides are used, they can provide a year-long curriculum series. Or if the guides are used in pairs, they can provide studies for a quarter (twelve weeks).

We want to emphasize that all of the guides in this series are designed to be useful to anyone. Each guide has a specific focus, but all are written with a general audience in mind. Additionally, the workbook format allows for personal interaction with biblical truths, making the guides adaptable to each individual's unique journey in recovery.

The four guides which all individuals and groups should find they can most easily relate to are *Recovery from Distorted Images of God, Recovery from Loss, Recovery from Bitterness* and *Recovery from Shame.* All of us need to replace our distorted images of God with biblically accurate images. All of us experience losses, disappointments and disillusionment in life, as well as loss through death or illness. We all have life experiences and relationships which lead to bitterness and which make forgiveness difficult. And we all experience shame and its debilitating consequences.

The four other guides are *Recovery from Codependency, Recovery from Family Dysfunctions, Recovery from Abuse* and *Recovery from Addictions.* Although these guides have a more specific focus, they address issues of very general concern both within the Christian community and in our culture as a whole. The biblical resources will be helpful to your recovery even if you do not share the specific concerns which these guides address.

Individuals who are working on a specific life issue and groups with a shared focus may want to begin with the guide which relates most directly to their concerns. Survivors of abuse, for example, may want to work through *Recovery from Abuse* and follow it with *Recovery from Shame.* Adult children from dysfunctional families may want to begin with *Recovery from Family Dysfunctions* and then use *Recovery from Distorted Images of God.* And those who struggle with addictive patterns may want to begin with *Recovery from Addictions* and then use *Recovery from Codependency.*

There are many other possibilities for study combinations. The short descriptions of each guide on the last page, as well as the information on the back of each guide will help you to further decide which guides will be most helpful to your recovery.

Preparing to Lead

1. Develop realistic expectations of yourself as a small group leader. Do not feel that you have to "have it all together." Rather, commit

yourself to an ongoing discipline of honesty about your own needs. As you grow in honesty about your own needs, you will grow as well in your capacity for compassion, gentleness and patience with yourself and with others. As a leader, you can encourage an atmosphere of honesty by being honest about yourself.

2. Pray. Pray for yourself and your own recovery. Pray for the group members. Invite the Holy Spirit to be present as you prepare and as you meet.

3. Read the study several times.

4. Take your time to thoughtfully work through each question, writing out your answers.

5. After completing your personal study, read through the leader's notes for the study you are leading. These notes are designed to help you in several ways. First, they tell you the purpose the authors had in mind while writing the study. Take time to think through how the questions work together to accomplish that purpose. Second, the notes provide you with additional background information or comments on some of the questions. This information can be useful if people have difficulty understanding or answering a question. Third, the leader's notes can alert you to potential problems you may encounter during the study.

6. If you wish to remind yourself during the group discussion of anything mentioned in the leader's notes, make a note to yourself below that question in your study guide.

Leading the Study

1. Begin on time. You may want to open in prayer, or have a group member do so.

2. Be sure everyone has a study guide. Decide as a group if you want people to do the study on their own ahead of time. If your time together is limited, it will be helpful for people to prepare in advance.

3. At the beginning of your first time together, explain that these studies are meant to be discussions, not lectures. Encourage the members of the group to participate. However, do not put pressure on those who may be hesitant to speak during the first few sessions. Clearly state that people do not need to share anything they do not feel safe sharing. Remind people that it will take time to trust each other.

4. Read aloud the group guidelines listed in the front of the guide. These commitments are important in creating a safe place for people to talk and trust and feel.

5. The covers of the Life Recovery Guides are designed to incorporate both symbols of the past and hope for the future. During your first meeting, allow the group to describe what they see in the cover and respond to it.

6. Read aloud the introductory paragraphs at the beginning of the discussion for the day. This will orient the group to the passage being studied.

7. The personal reflection questions are designed to help group members focus on some aspect of their experience. Hopefully, they will help group members to be more aware of the frame of reference and life experience which they bring to the study. The personal reflection section can be done prior to the group meeting or as the first part of the meeting. If the group does not prepare in advance, approximately ten minutes will be needed for individuals to consider these questions.

The personal reflection questions are not designed to be used directly for group discussion. Rather, the first question in the Bible study section is intended to give group members an opportunity to reveal what they feel safe sharing from their time of personal reflection.

8. Read the passage aloud. You may choose to do this yourself, or prior to the study you might ask someone else to read.

9. As you begin to ask the questions in the guide, keep several things in mind. First, the questions are designed to be used just as they are written. If you wish, you may simply read them aloud to the group.

Or you may prefer to express them in your own words. However, unnecessary rewording of the questions is not recommended.

Second, the questions are intended to guide the group toward understanding and applying the main idea of the study. You will find the purpose of each study described in the leader's notes. You should try to understand how the study questions and the biblical text work together to lead the group in that direction.

There may be times when it is appropriate to deviate from the study guide. For example, a question may have already been answered. If so, move on to the next question. Or someone may raise an important question not covered in the guide. Take time to discuss it! The important thing is to use discretion. There may be many routes you can travel to reach the goal of the study. But the easiest route is usually the one we have suggested.

10. Don't be afraid of silence. People need time to think about the question before formulating their answers.

11. Draw out a variety of responses from the group. Ask, "Who else has some thoughts about this?" or "How did some of the rest of you respond?" until several people have given answers to the question.

12. Acknowledge all contributions. Try to be affirming whenever possible. Never reject an answer. If it seems clearly wrong to you, ask, "Which part of the text led you to that conclusion?" or "What do the rest of you think?"

13. Realize that not every answer will be addressed to you, even though this will probably happen at first. As group members become more at ease, they will begin to interact more effectively with each other. This is a sign of a healthy discussion.

14. Don't be afraid of controversy. It can be very stimulating. Differences can enrich our lives. If you don't resolve an issue completely, don't be frustrated. Move on and keep it in mind for later. A subsequent study may resolve the problem. Or, the issue may not be resolved—not all questions have answers!

15. Stick to the passage under consideration. It should be the source for answering the questions. Discourage the group from unnecessary cross-referencing. Likewise, stick to the subject and avoid going off on tangents.

16. Periodically summarize what the group has said about the topic. This helps to draw together the various ideas mentioned and gives continuity to the study. But be careful not to use summary statements as an opportunity to give a sermon!

17. During the discussion, feel free to share your own responses. Your honesty about your own recovery can set a tone for the group to feel safe in sharing. Be careful not to dominate the time, but do allow time for your own needs as a group member.

18. Each study ends with a time for prayer. There are several ways to handle this time in a group. The person who leads each study could lead the group in a prayer or you could allow time for group participation. Remember that some members of your group may feel uncomfortable about participating in public prayer. It might be helpful to discuss this with the group during your first meeting and to reach some agreement about how to proceed.

19. Realize that trust in a group grows over time. During the first couple meetings, people will be assessing how safe they will feel in the group. Do not be discouraged if people share only superficially at first. The level of trust will grow slowly but steadily.

Listening to Emotional Pain

Life Recovery Guides are designed to take seriously the pain and struggle that is part of life. People will experience a variety of emotions during these studies. Your role as group leader is not to act as a professional counselor. Instead it is to be a friend who listens to emotional pain. Listening is a gift you can give to hurting people. For many, it is not an easy gift to give. The following suggestions can help you listen more effectively to people in emotional pain.

1. Remember that you are not responsible to take the pain away. People in helping relationships often feel that they are being asked

to make the other person feel better. This is usually related to the helper's own patterns of not being comfortable with painful feelings.
2. Not only are you not responsible to take the pain away, one of the things people need most is an opportunity to face and to experience the pain in their lives. They have usually spent years denying their pain and running from it. Healing can come when we are able to face our pain in the presence of someone who cares about us. Rather than trying to take the pain away, commit yourself to listening attentively as it is expressed.
3. Realize that some group members may not feel comfortable with expressions of sadness or anger. You may want to acknowledge that such emotions are uncomfortable, but remind the group that part of recovery is to learn to feel and to allow others to feel.
4. Be very cautious about giving answers and advice. Advice and answers may make you feel better or feel competent, but they may also minimize people's problems and their painful feelings. Simple solutions rarely work, and they can easily communicate "You should be better now" or "You shouldn't really be talking about this."
5. Be sure to communicate direct affirmation any time people talk about their painful emotions. It takes courage to talk about our pain because it creates anxiety for us. It is a great gift to be trusted by those who are struggling.

The following notes refer to the questions in the Bible study portion of each study:

Study 1. Letting Go of Over-Responsibility. Exodus 18:13-24.
Purpose: To learn to let go of over-responsibility.
Question 2. First, there was a problem with limited access to the legal process: "People stand around you from morning till evening." Second, Moses was under a great deal of stress. Third, others with leadership abilities were not being given an opportunity to develop these abilities.
Question 3. Jethro is not trying to manipulate Moses. He does not

say "You're doing such a wonderful job, but there's this one little thing." Jethro puts the bottom line in his first sentence: "What you are doing is not good." Additionally, Jethro does not verbally abuse Moses or shame him. He does not call him stupid, grandiose or proud. He doesn't say, "Moses you are always making mistakes like this." He simply addresses the problem. Finally, Jethro says, "I will give you some advice, and may God be with you." He is leaving the outcome with God.

Question 4. Read carefully the way Moses explains his behavior. His first sentence distracts attention from the concerns raised by Jethro and blames the people. Moses presents himself both as a helpless victim of circumstances and as the only person in Israel capable of giving guidance about God's laws.

Question 5. Moses no doubt experienced a number of losses during this transition. Trusting other people means less control and power. Moses described business-as-usual as "It is brought to me, and I decide." Losing that kind of control and authority would not be easy for any of us.

Moses also lost the personal satisfactions and the social rewards for codependent behavior that come when people believe the myth that a person is irreplaceable. No doubt Moses was admired for his competence, productivity and "superhuman" strength. It is important to remember that, even though these rewards are rooted in myths that cannot be sustained, when we lose a myth it is a real loss. Making the transition to more participatory rule required Moses to grieve these losses.

Question 6. Other capable leaders were identified and allowed to serve. Moses no longer had to do it all. And the people were much better served.

Study 2. Letting God Give Us Rest. Matthew 11:28-30.
Purpose: To learn to let God give us rest.
Question 2. Some people may see the good news in this text imme-

diately. People caught up in codependent behaviors are weary as a result of the heavy burdens they carry for others. At some level we all know that we need rest.

Many people may, however, see invitations to relationship as invitations to anything but rest. We believe things like: "If I get involved with you, I will lose myself. If I let you know who I am, you will reject me. Or, I'll have to work very hard to take care of you in order to earn your love." These beliefs keep us on guard in relationships, even our relationship with God.

Others may read this text as if it were an invitation only to people who are much more weary and much more burdened than themselves. There is always someone whose situation is worse than ours. But this mentality keeps us from accepting the help and comfort we need.

Question 3. One way to avoid seeing ourselves as needy, burdened people is to keep busy. People living in a frenzy can avoid, at least for a while, facing the painful emotions which begin to surface in moments of quiet. For this reason Sunday (intended by God for rest) is for many people one of the most heavily programmed days of the week. Vacations (intended for renewal) often become as tightly scheduled and as full of events as our normal schedules. Encourage group members to talk about the anxieties which keep them from accepting God's invitation to rest.

Question 4. Our ability to rest (that is, relax and "be ourselves") with a person is largely dependent on our convictions about the character of the person. If we see God as demanding, judging or abusive, it will be extremely difficult to imagine ever resting in his presence. Who could rest in the presence of someone who demands perfection and is eager to remind you of every one of your mistakes? It is this image of God that leads us to compulsive religious behaviors and over-responsibility.

Jesus' description of himself as one who is gentle and humble probably will come as a surprise to some people. It is a picture of someone who would accept us, welcome us, love us and value us for who we are rather than merely for what we do. God's gentleness and humility allow us to let down our defenses and be open to his love.

Question 5. Few codependent people can make much sense out of faith that is easy. We expect faith to be another arena for our compulsivity. It's as if we say to God: "Just tell me how bad I am, then I will do anything you say. In fact, I'll do it compulsively, and we'll both be fine. I'll be too busy being faithful to have time to feel anything, and you won't have to be bothered with me." Notice how this leaves us pretty much in control of the relationship (which is how we like it) and allows us to sustain our denial system. Big burdens? No problem. We can handle it.

What a contrast this text is to our compulsive/addictive approaches to faith! Jesus invites us to "soul rest." Denial is an enormous burden; it offers no rest. You have to spend energy every day, all day, to sustain denial. Facing our neediness may not seem easy, but it opens the possibility for genuine rest, deep rest, rest for our souls.

Study 3. Letting Go of Denial. Psalm 102:1-11, 17-20.
Purpose: To learn to let go of denial.

Question 2. This psalm was most likely written during a time of national distress, perhaps during the Babylonian exile. It describes the writer's personal distress in the midst of national disaster.

"Blighted and withered like grass" is a picture of death. Codependent behavior often results in a kind of emotional numbness. It leaves a person so focused on others that no time remains for development of self-awareness or for pursuing personal growth. As a result, codependence can lead to an emotional and spiritual death.

Question 3. The picture is of someone who is on guard, unable to sleep, facing the struggles of life alone, like a person who cannot sleep at night. Instead of sleeping, the person paces the floor consumed with worry, unable to enjoy life because of someone else's behavior, feeling utterly alone.

Question 4. Codependent behavior is focused on changing, helping or "fixing" another person. These efforts are largely futile, but nevertheless become, for many people, a compulsive preoccupation. The compulsivity and the helplessness of the task lead people to feel trapped, powerless, and, hopefully, in need of a power greater than themselves to restore them to sanity.

Question 5. The descriptions include bones that burn, and the writer is forgetting to eat, groaning loudly and crying. Encourage the group to compare the writer's experience with their own experiences of physical and emotional distress.

Question 6. The emotional distress of codependence is accompanied by spiritual distress. It feels like God does not care or that he is unwilling to help. We ask God to change the other person only to discover that he wants us to change. Encourage people to compare the writer's experience of spiritual distress with their own experiences.

Question 8. You may want to read this aloud slowly for the group and allow them time to write a response before you talk about responses to this image.

Study 4. Letting God Help Us Tell the Truth. Matthew 18:15-17.
Purpose: To learn to let God help us be honest in relationships.

Question 2. The key points are (1) Jesus assumes that we will be sinned against and that it is important to recognize this when it happens; (2) conflict can be addressed directly and honestly; (3) there are a variety of approaches to conflict resolution that can be tried; (4) outside help may be needed; and (5) we may not achieve the outcome we hope for. The point here is not to lay out a universally applicable strategy for conflict management, but rather to summarize what is wise in conflict situations. Rigid step-by-step application of these approaches to every situation would not necessarily be helpful.

Question 3. In dysfunctional social systems people often talk to everyone except the person who has hurt them. This tends to decrease trust. Others think, "If they say this behind Joe's back, what will they say behind my back?" It adds to the sense of helplessness in the group or family because the people who could do something about the problem aren't talking about it. It also adds to the general level of inappropriate over-responsibility in the group because everybody is asked to worry about other people's business without being able to address the problem directly.

It is important to add that seeking wise counsel from a close friend or counselor can be an important first step in preparing yourself to talk directly with someone who has hurt you. It is the pattern of talking to third parties without ever seeking to talk with the person who has hurt you that can be damaging.

Question 4. The fears that keep us from direct and honest communication are many. The person may not respond; we may fear that we will hurt the other person, or we may fear that they will hurt us. It is also difficult to admit we are vulnerable to being hurt. And, it is difficult to make ourselves vulnerable again to the person who hurt us.

Question 5. The text says that direct, honest communication can often "win your brother over." The problem can be identified and discussed. Depending on the nature of the offending person's behavior, a private conversation can allow that person the opportunity to hear that a problem exists, to listen to the complaint, to lower his or her defenses enough to see the situation from the other person's perspective, to share his or her own perspective and/or to ask for forgiveness.

Question 6. In some situations in which we have been sinned against, it may be wise to involve a pastor or counselor from the start. This may be an important step for us to even identify that there is a problem and what it is. It can also be a critical second step, after a private conversation with the person, because it can provide the perspective, knowledge or support we need to continue to attempt to resolve the problem.

Question 7. Conflict management is not one of the strong points of most local churches. It is important to remember that when Jesus gave this advice the church was not a well-organized institution but a community of believers. Jesus is not envisioning that people would stand up during a worship service and tell the congregation how they have been sinned against!

Jesus, however, did anticipate that the community of his followers would have some meaningful role to play in conflict resolution. The reason for this is that it is not too difficult for us to stack the deck if all we need to find are two or three witnesses. Thus, the point of telling the church is not to make everything public, but rather to submit the matter to arbitration by parties not intimately connected with the conflict. In our situations this might involve finding a pastor, counselor or congregational leader to help with conflict resolution or seeking mediation services from organizations such as the Christian Legal Society.

Question 8. Jesus most emphatically does not mean "treat them like dirt." Jesus developed a reputation for associating with pagans and tax collectors! The point here is that our expectations should change. We will need to let go of our demands and work on our own recovery, even if the other person chooses never to change.

Study 5. Letting Go of Blame. Genesis 3:1-13.

Purpose: To learn to let go of blame.

Question 2. They hid because they were afraid and because they were naked. Notice that the man explains what happened in terms of fear and exposure. Blame is a way of protecting ourselves against things we fear and it is a way of "covering" ourselves when we sense we are vulnerable. The experiences of fear and exposure are the emotional roots of blame.

Question 3. Blame is a way of protecting ourselves when we feel exposed and afraid. It is a way of hiding out, much like physically hiding among the trees. Blame keeps us from facing the truth and from feeling our pain, making us feel powerful when we really feel weak. Blame is sustained by the myth that everything would be fine if the other person were different. We all find it convenient to avoid personal responsibility and blame makes that possible.

Victims of verbal, physical or sexual abuse may need to spend some extra time talking about the concept of blame. An important part of recovery from abuse is recognizing who was responsible for the abuse. Responsibility for the abuse must be clearly given to the abuser. Giving back responsibility for abuse, however, is not the same as blaming. Unlike blame, returning responsibility to the appropriate person brings clarity, allowing us to face the truth and acknowledge our feelings including our intense anger and deep grief. It releases abusers to grow or not grow depending on their own choices. For victims, blame is saying, "It's all your fault, I am absolutely helpless unless you change." Recovery comes from saying, "I am not responsible for what you did to me; I am responsible for my own recovery; and I am free to grow and change no matter what you choose."

Question 4. Because blame keeps us from facing the truth about ourselves, change is not possible. Blame is a dead-end strategy because everything depends on other people. And, often, these "other people" give no indication that they consider change to be desirable.

Question 5. Being blamed can be a very confusing experience. You feel devalued, shut out, defensive. It feels terrible to be blamed. And, more importantly, it doesn't help to resolve things. Instead it creates additional problems.

Question 6. To let go of blame would mean to face the fear and the exposure that blame covers. These are emotionally painful experiences. To let go of blame is to let go of a sense of control and power.

Question 7. Blame, whether of others or ourselves, is moralistic, simplistic, judgmental and without mercy, grace or love. Our goal is not to blame ourselves rather than blaming others. The goal is to let go of blame entirely so that we can take appropriate responsibility for our own recovery.

Question 8. For some people, blame is such a deeply ingrained response to life's difficulties that alternatives may not be obvious. Remember that blame is often the end product of several generations of family dysfunction.

Among the things that are more helpful than blame are: facing our failure, accepting our limits, accepting God's continuing love for us, realizing that no failure is final, accepting the things we can't change, and taking the responsibility to change the things that are within our power to change.

Study 6. Letting God Take Care of Those We Love. Mark 10:17-23.
Purpose: To learn to trust God to take care of the consequences of other people's behavior.

Question 2. He is wealthy. He is a devout, religious person who is respectful of Jesus as a teacher. Jesus does not dispute his assertion of faithfulness to the law.

Question 4. Notice that there is no hint in this text of frantic attempts to convince the man that he has made the wrong choice. Jesus answered the man's question honestly. He respected the man's right to make a choice, and he let him live with the consequences of his decision. Jesus sees him leaving and turns to his disciples to interpret this event for them. He acknowledges the difficult decision which the man faced and the generality of the problem. Jesus let him go.

Question 5. Letting go of someone you love leads to grief. And it is the painful reality of grief that we are trying to avoid when we try to control, manipulate or protect other people from the consequences of their decisions. Grief may be a painful emotion, but it is based in reality.

Question 6. A typical codependent response would be to try anything to get this man to respond. We would negotiate the terms: "O.K., maybe only a generous contribution. Would that be acceptable?" We might run after him asking, "Maybe you just need a little time to think about it, can we talk again tomorrow." We might attempt to shame the man into responding by asking, "How could you be so foolish?" It would be difficult for us to respect him enough and to trust God enough to let him go.

Question 7. Letting go is important for our own spiritual and mental health, but it is also extremely important for the dignity and freedom of the other person. Manipulating, controlling, shaming and modifying consequences can keep people from looking seriously at what they want and need in life. As a result, choices often aren't real choices, commitments aren't real commitments. Allowing for real freedom gives people the gift of experiencing love without control. It gives them the freedom to make honest commitments and changes.

For more information about Christian resources for people in recovery and subscription information for STEPS, *the newsletter of the National Association for Christian Recovery, we invite you to write to:*

The National Association for Christian Recovery
P.O. Box 11095
Whittier, California 90603

LIFE RECOVERY GUIDES FROM INTER-VARSITY PRESS
By Dale and Juanita Ryan

Recovery from Abuse. Does the nightmare of abuse ever end? After emotional, verbal and/or physical abuse how can you develop secure relationships? Recovery is difficult but possible. This guide will help you turn to God as you put the broken pieces of your life back together again. Six studies, 64 pages, 1158-3.

Recovery from Addictions. Addictions have always been part of the human predicament. Chemicals, food, people, sex, work, spending, gambling, religious practices and more can enslave us. This guide will help you find the wholeness and restoration that God offers to those who are struggling with addictions. Six studies, 64 pages, 1155-9.

Recovery from Bitterness. Sometimes forgiveness gets blocked, stuck, restrained and entangled. We find our hearts turning toward bitterness and revenge. Our inability to forgive can make us feel like spiritual failures. This guide will help us find the strength to change bitterness into forgiveness. Six studies, 64 pages, 1154-0.

Recovery from Codependency. The fear, anger and helplessness people feel when someone they love is addicted can lead to desperate attempts to take care of, or control, the loved one. Both the addicted person's behavior and the frenzied codependent behavior progress in a destructive downward spiral of denial and blame. This guide will help you to let go of over-responsibility and entrust the people you love to God. Six studies, 64 pages, 1156-7.

Recovery from Distorted Images of God. In a world of sin and hate it is difficult for us to understand who the God of love is. These distortions interfere with our ability to express our feelings to God and to trust him. This guide helps us to identify the distortions we have and to come to a new understanding of who God is. Six studies, 64 pages, 1152-4.

Recovery from Family Dysfunctions. Dysfunctional patterns of relating learned early in life affect all of our relationships. We trust God and others less than we wish. This guide offers healing from the pain of the past and acceptance into God's family. Six studies, 64 pages, 1151-6.

Recovery from Loss. Disappointment, unmet expectations, physical or emotional illness and death are all examples of losses that occur in our lives. Working through grief does not help us to forget what we have lost, but it does help us grow in understanding, compassion and courage in the midst of loss. This guide will show you how to receive the comfort God offers. Six studies, 64 pages, 1157-5.

Recovery from Shame. Shame is a social experience. Whatever its source, shame causes people to see themselves as unloveable, unworthy and irreparable. This guide will help you to reform your self-understanding in the light of God's unconditional acceptance. Six studies, 64 pages, 1153-2.